Simple Thoughts - Simple Pleasures
Color Your World With Words

Cynthia "Cookie" Viloria

authorHOUSE

AuthorHouse™
1663 Liberty Drive
Bloomington, IN 47403
www.authorhouse.com
Phone: 833-262-8899

© 2009 Cynthia "Cookie" Viloria. All rights reserved.

No part of this book may be reproduced, stored in a retrieval system, or transmitted by any means without the written permission of the author.

Published by AuthorHouse 09/19/2022

ISBN: 978-1-4389-8933-4 (sc)
ISBN: 978-1-4389-8934-1 (hc)
ISBN: 978-1-4389-8935-8 (e)

Print information available on the last page.

Any people depicted in stock imagery provided by Getty Images are models, and such images are being used for illustrative purposes only.
Certain stock imagery © Getty Images.

This book is printed on acid-free paper.

Because of the dynamic nature of the Internet, any web addresses or links contained in this book may have changed since publication and may no longer be valid. The views expressed in this work are solely those of the author and do not necessarily reflect the views of the publisher, and the publisher hereby disclaims any responsibility for them.

A Tribute

Cynthia Marie "Cookie" Tyre Viloria
was a loving wife, sister, niece, aunt and friend.

Cynthia worked tirelessly on bringing this work to the point of publication. She had the rare ability to put feelings and thoughts into beautiful words. Sadly, on July 30, 2009, she passed away after a short illness.

A Couple's Love

The life of a couple should be lived with each other in mind.
It is so necessary to display an attitude that is loving and kind.
Of course, no one is as close to you than your husband or your wife.
Work to rule out discord, and strife.

This person you married has to be your life long friend.
You vowed to stay together to the very end.
Hand in hand, through good times and bad.
You've made your house into a home, a lovely little pad.

Life is full of challenges and hurdles to get over.
Allow your deepest love, misunderstandings and hurt feelings, to cover.
These test and trials can make you all the more strong.
That is such a help when things appear to go wrong.

Instilled in you is an inborn desire to please each other.
Due to your love, respect, and admiration, it is no bother.
You finally see you are no longer two, but one.
A selfish, independent attitude you wisely shun.

Continue growing closer and be glad of who you are.
From the shy couple, you have come so far.
Forever think of him as he thinks of you.
Moments of unhappiness will be quite few.

A Friend Indeed

It is so nice to have friends.
They will stick with you to the end.
Fair weather friends will come and go.
There is substance to their friendship, and it shows.
A true friend is someone you laugh with, cry with and together grow.
When tides and weather changes, they help to shield the blows.
You find yourself giggling at the silliest things.
And into your life new and beneficial viewpoints they bring.
Constantly thinking of your feelings before their own.
They season their words with salt when telling you that you're wrong.
To be a lifelong friend, both persons have to give.
Of energy, and time to make life enjoyable to live.
It is a relationship that needs tender loving care.
Like two peas in a pod, you're the perfect pair.

A Mother's Love

A mother's love can not be measured by possessions.
There are no measurements for the happiness she brings.
She will put herself out just to make sure her child has what it needs.
A self-sacrificing spirit and an endless love she has.
Also a spirit that loves to nurture and cuddle the heart.
When this new little one enters the world, no one considers them more precious than their mothers.
Even as we grow older, they know exactly what to say or do to make her child feel better.
I found it so comforting to snuggle with my mother while chatting.
Although we feel ourselves to be plain and ordinary, to our mothers, we are beautiful.
To us they are our pride and joy, and we would give our last to make them happy.
They are full of sunshine, rainbows, and stars, so bright and magnificent.
Let's take care of them and make them feel as special as they surely are.

A Scenic Backyard in Autumn

Standing here watching the trees changing.
How beautiful to look upon.
Colors of every description, so bright,
Green, yellow, red, and even burgundy.
The lawn, all carpeted with leaves.
In my mind I imagine children at play.
They are rolling tumbling and feeling free.
Can you hear their laughter?
Can you see their puppy frolicking too?
Oh how relaxing to behold.
Just below these fallen leaves is a slow
Running river.
Sitting on the deck overlooking boats and
Kayaks slowly rolling along.
A lovely breeze blowing through.
The scene is one of serenity.
Autumn here is peaceful, colorful, and nostalgic.
Not only are there sounds of children, there are
Also sounds of birds chirping.
There are sounds of bees gathering the last pollen of
The season.
Towering trees with squirrels leaping from tree to tree.
Life here in this backyard never ceases.
Look upon it with joy. A boat dock to sit on that gives you
The feeling of being adrift on the water.
Pick your favorite book and read.
Take an afternoon to be engulfed in it.

Single Girl's Prayer

I am a single girl but I do not complain.
Disquieting thoughts I try to refrain.
It's difficult at times to be alone.
To Jehovah above, I let it be known.
Now I work on qualities that will make me better.
With faith and conviction, any storm I can weather.
Yet a mate for myself is what I desire.
I pray that I stand strong and never tire.
Someone for me to share my space,
I close my eyes to see his face.
Right now I do not see him so clear,
But when I do, I promise to hold him dear.
I want to be the best wife I can be.
I keep it in prayer, Jehovah hear my plea.
In harmony with my prayers I constantly try.
Simplicity in life, I keep before my eyes.
A love to walk with and someone to talk to,
These feelings sublime and o' so new.
He is surely out there, for it is my hearts desire.
It's not necessary for me to pass out flyers.
In due time I will reap, so I will not tire out.
Not even sit in my room, to sulk and pout.
They are always new friends to be made.
Friendships with lasting foundations laid.
So until the face of my mate is clearly seen,
Leaving him in Jehovah God's hands, I am surely keen.

A SOFT VOICE

Do you hear that soft voice from behind you?
It's so very soft as the color's soft hue.
From you, it is never far away.
Always there to wish you a good day.
Throughout the day you hear hard sounds.
Harsh words in your ears that constantly pound.
Now take a moment and listen to the softness of my voice.
It's up to you though, you have a choice.
There's beauty in a gentle breeze.
There's beauty in the sway of trees.
Relax your mind and daydream of a quiet intimate park.
Just you and I, and we are happy as a lark.
So beautiful and colorful the flowers are.
In this park there's not even a car.
Only beauty, peace and serenity.
Fruits so sweet and of the best quality.
Allow this beauty to replenish your zest.
This you truly need when put to the test.
We need that soft voice and place of escape.
Ponder on the bright colors and picturesque landscape.
So when things are stressful and you are blue,
Listen! Did you hear it? That soft voice from behind you.

A Stressed Out World

Faces showing discomfort and stress
People just don't smile anymore, not even to themselves.
It use to be a pleasant look could make one smile.
Now you smile and it's returned with a grimace.
Life is so difficult now-a-days.
The necessities of life are becoming more difficult to have.
Luxuries aren't the main notion now.
Some don't know where their next meal will come from.
Elderly ones are freezing right in their own homes.
There are senior citizens that are eating dog food because it is cheap.
This system is in need for a complete over-haul.
It will come in the very near future.
It is not in the hand of man to make this change.
Only our heavenly Father can and will do this.
It will be for the betterment of man.

A Vow

A vow I'm making to only you of my love, respect, loyalty, and devotion.
To be here for you when you need.
To give you encouragement to feel.
To share with you happiness in times of despair.
To be your solace when you need comforting.
When the sun is shining so brightly,
I will be there to bottle it up for a rainy day.
Then, of course, to be there for you to love whenever you need.
And to be loved by you so tenderly.

I vow to you my constant effort to make our marriage as wonderful as it can be.
To give to you my feelings, my intimate thoughts, my desires, hopes, and dreams.
To be by your side, to listen to you, is also my vow.

With all else that I vow to you, I vow to you, ME, solely for you, to have and to hold today and forevermore.

A Wintry Day - Quiet Thoughts

The coolness of a winter's day
How refreshing to see trees as they sway
Or hear the laughter of a child at play
All bundled up by a mom who would say
"Have fun in the yard, and there you stay"

Little cheeks and noses so rosy and red
After a nice hot bath, it's off to bed
Dreaming of teddy bears and kittens, no dread
Their round little tummies are full and well fed
Loving parents there to protect them from being afraid

A new day dawns with wintry skies
Grass that was green now dries
Pine combs and leaves fall and dies
Winter is now here and South the birds flies
Winds billowing and whistling like subtle cries

Morning we awaken to heavy dew
Sneezing, coughing, or runny noses to name a few
Are the winter's effects on you and me, too
The harshness of some winters will make you exclaim," phew"
Snow begins to fall and gradually accrue

Yards and trees are white as a sheet
So eager to make snow cream to eat
On the side of a hill, friends we meet
To have a go on our sleds out in the streets
Then rushing inside to get close to the heat
Winters may be cold, but still are very nice

Yet to nature, it pays the price
All snug as a bug, are the field mice
Sneaking about looking for a cheese slice
They, too, as nature surely pay a high price

Winters, oh yes, so lovely, they are
Better to look at from inside your house or your car
It's effects are felt both near and far
Sometimes, making us not feel quite up to par
But how beautiful are the gleaming,
And glistening wintry stars

AM I YOUR IDEAL WOMAN

Must we all be that perfect size
Must we all be that perfect height
Must we all be that perfect weight
To be counted as beautiful?

Do we have to have long flowing hair
Do we have to be fair skinned
Do we have to have thin lips
Just to be counted as attractive?

If my eye lashes were longer
If my teeth were whiter or straighter
If my nose was smaller
Would that make me prettier?

Maybe if my breast were larger
Maybe if my legs were longer
Maybe if my hips were less round
Could I be considered cute?

Sadly this is the thinking of many.
But it's not a scale for everyone.
Some are not so shallow.
Some are not just surface viewers.

All are bestowed with a beauty from within ourselves.
No one can take that from us.
Your personality and attitude makes you, YOU.
Beautiful personalities lend to beautiful people.

I've seen models that were "beautiful."
Yet when they began to speak, they lose their "beauty."
Some are self-centered, arrogant, and opinionated.
Again they've loss their beauty, their prettiness.

Being the girl next door isn't always bad.
Sometimes she has more going for her
Than that highly paid model.
Beauty comes in all packages, all sizes, colors, and all nationalities.

Look for that true beauty from within.
It's there. I promise you.
Hold on to it, never let it go.
YOU are BEAUTIFUL.

AUTUMN - A TIME TO REFLECT

Take a moment to stop and reflect on calm waters, picturesque
scenes, your thoughts collect.
Do you hear the sound of a babbling brook?
Colors, so crisp, so gold, around every crook.

A sunset so lovely with orange and purple hues.
Don't give way to thoughts of this world's bad news.
Close your eyes and ponder on a glassy lake.
Drink in its beauty and deep breaths you take.

Hills and mountains covered with Fall trees.
Late in the evening there's a gentle breeze.
Give yourself an escape to bring peace to your soul.
Stressful times can surely take their toll.

Now take time to share this with a mate.
Autumn is my time of the year for such a date.
Hand in hand, as you enjoy the trails.
Gleaning the serenity, every intricate detail.

Commune with nature, enjoy it to the full.
Allow it on your heart to tug, to pull.
The Autumn is my special time of the year.
It fills my very being with cheer.

BE AS A CHILD

Look at things through the eyes of a child
The simplicity, the colors, so uncomplicated
No negativity's are there with children
They look at things bright and new

How innocent, not knowing of prejudices
Always full of smiles and beaming eyes
Not knowing dread or fearing harm
Forever eager to give and receive love

Children learn from adults whose hearts have been reshaped
Prejudices, acts of hatred, and harshness they are taught
These hurtful things will follow this child's life
Only if they are taught right from you, will it help

Be as a child when it comes to badness
Maintain this innocence for all time
Keep an open mind and think of the other person first
We can be wise right now
Yet with the heart of a child

BE CONTENT WITH WHO YOU ARE

Don't look down on someone because they are not your ideal style.
Running one down to others, revealing a hidden jealousy, all the while.
We are all endowed with qualities and attributes worth being proud of.
One personality trait we should cultivate is that of love.
It does not matter your size, color, stature or height.
We all add our own facets to the circle of life.
Husbands and wives share their own special talents.
Together they relate, forming a balance.
Such a blessing it is, that there is much variety on the earth.
Imagine how boring it would be if we all looked the same at birth.
Deep inside us, we have a hidden gift.
Take a moment and find yours, it will give you a lift.

THE BEAUTY OF THE NIGHT

Imagine setting under a starlit sky
Many stars twinkling against a blanket
So deep, so dark, so black, and still so very beautiful
The night falls and the sounds suddenly change
The sound of wind blowing through trees
Or rushing falling leaves
If you listen, it sounds as if it is greeting you, and
Welcoming the close of another awesome day
So still the night is, as darkness envelopes what the
Darkness has left behind
There is tranquility in the night, unlike anything
One has ever experienced
Nothing compares to it's brilliance
The heavenly bodies hanging there so wonderfully
Unhurried, and so unchangeable
How could it's beauty ever be compared
There is just no way, no words of conveying it's uniqueness
Amazing beauty of a full moon against a darken sky
Have you ever watched a full moon over a body of water
Shining and shimmering
It's like millions of tiny diamonds, all reflecting
The brilliance of each other
Most frequently our minds drift to someone we love
In wanting to share such loveliness with them
Reflecting on such beauty is invigorating to ones soul
There's so much beauty in the night
Use your imagination and dream
Dream of pleasant days gone by and of relaxing
Days to come
It's all a part of the circle of life

BECAUSE I WANT TO

You ask me why I give so much of myself to you.
BECAUSE I WANT TO.
You ask me why I allow you to lean on me for support.
BECAUSE I WANT TO.
You ask me why I speak to you in my funny but loving way.
BECAUSE I WANT TO.
You ask me why I'm so sensitive to the needs of others.
BECAUSE I WANT TO.

I want to be your shade on a hot sunny day.
I want to be your quiet escape from your noisy everyday surroundings.
I want to be your companion and helper for the rest of our lives.
I want to be your spotlight defining your many fine qualities.
I want to be your confidant when you need to talk.
I want to fill your empty days and nights with joy and happiness.
All the things I do, all the things I say, all the things I share with you, Why?
BECAUSE I WANT TO.

BEING CLOSE TO YOU

Being with you makes me feel so safe and warm.
It's comforting know you will protect me from harm.
When I run to you with little things you are not alarmed.
You have so much love, kindness, and charm.

I look into your eyes and see just how much you care.
Your love and devotion, you constantly declare.
We enjoy reading things and with each other share.
Finding a friend and companion like you is so rare.

Just being close to you or feeling your touch, really makes me love
and appreciate you so much.
A brother, gentle, sweet, and respectful as such, with your words, my
heart you have touched.

I long for a chance to share your space.
To be held in your arms and to touch your face.
We've come this far, now we'll finish the race.
I'm waiting and looking forward to your warm embrace.

From the moment that I heard your voice,
I knew deep from within, you were my choice.
When our paths crossed, I thanked God and sincerely rejoiced.
While I'm alone, in my head and mind, I replay your voice.

Being close to you, at play and at rest,
I love being able to rest my head on your chest.
My arms are opened to you. Our love for each other we manifest.
Holding you in my arms is for me the very best.

BREATHE - JUST BREATHE

When you feel anxious and confused take a moment to take a deep breath and breathe.
Sometimes curves are thrown into our regular routine of life.
Feelings of being overwhelmed or being in a pressure cooker begins to rise.
Stop and breathe.
For those days that you wake up and although it's Wednesday it feels like a Monday.
Rise to an aromatic cup of coffee.
Inhale deeply, just breathe.
Ever so often tempers may flair and for whatever reason the disturbance, walk away.
Close your eyes and breathe from the stomach.
Appreciate every day, every minute, come what may.
The ability to move, think, speak, and even touch our loved ones.
Some are not as blessed as you and are denied that privilege.
So spend a bit of time to ponder on the positive and breathe. Just breathe.

BRIDLED THOUGHTS

The sun is so bright this morning.
Birds are chirping and singing.
The air smells sweet as if perfume is in the air.
Just glancing out of the window and there's a mama rabbit and her baby rabbit.
They are obviously getting their morning started.
And there is a quiet calm in the area.
I don't even hear a car passing by, not even the dogs are noisy at play.
Maybe it's time for all to take a quiet moment to regroup.
Talking to oneself while meditating.
Use the time to reflect on things you want to accomplish and by what means you will make it happen.
Thoughts of whose life will you touch today, or whose day will you make brighter.
Every moment of every day is a gift.
Don't squander it, use it to the full.
Rise to subdued moments.
Bridled thoughts.

CHOCOLATE

It is smooth and sweet at times.
Other times it is dark and delectably tart.
Comes in so many shapes and sizes.
And, of course, it leaves a smile on your face.

Now what on earth could this ever be?
I will give you a hint, it is truly a woman's comfort, and every man realizes that.

Do you know what it is now?
If you answered flowers, no not this time, not even roses.
Could it be jewelry, diamonds?

That pick me up for ladies is, "Chocolate."
Nothing replaces a good chocolate bar.
Dark chocolate has been known to be healthy for you.
Now they even have white chocolate.

On those days when you're just not feeling your best, go ahead and have a piece.
French chocolates are so tasty and divine.
I think I'll have a chocolate right now.

WE ARE NEVER CRAMPED BEYOND MOVEMENT

When cramped, He promises to bring us into a "roomy place"
Feelings of stress and discomfort, He will erase.

Daily Jehovah will "carry our load."
Rich blessing from him has always flowed.

He can see our hearts, what we truly desire.
Our zeal for him, inside us is like a "fire."

Yet human's tendencies toward stress can deem our "light."
From isolating ourselves may we forever fight!

Talk to Jehovah constantly, every day.
He will help us never to stray.

So if we're sensitive to Jehovah, just as his eyes
Surely when we're stressed he hears our cries.

So before Jehovah we lay down our cares.
Before him our souls we bare.

He will help you, he will, just as he's helped me.
From overwhelming anxieties, he's set me free.

.

DAYS GONE BY

People rushing to and fro.
Tired bodies and hurting feet to show.
Gone are the unrushed melancholy days.
Faces of stress as mothers nerves fray.

Energy levels wane as we age.
Little ones bouncing about at this stage.
How intriguing to look at things through their eyes.
Big smiles saying their "Hello", and "Bye Byes".

No one takes time to stop and listen to the songs of birds.
Computers, registers, and selling pitches are heard.
Gone are the days of enjoyable work.
Corruption and dishonesty around the corner lurks.

There is much more to life and living than what meets the eye.
Pondering on the beauty of nature makes us sigh.
How nice it would be to slow down the pace.
All this beauty around us embrace.

DEEP IN THOUGHT

As the night is long
Appreciate the shining stars
How they illuminate the sky
Always in perfect harmony

As the seasons are short
The warmth of the summer
The coolness of the Spring
The colors of the Fall

As the oceans are blue
Flowing gently with the tide
How beautiful the mountains
As their trees change appearance

Ponder on the little things
Truly clearing ones mind
Daydream of quiet moments
Reflect on inner peace

DEEP THOUGHTS - CLOUDS

Clouds rushing by, ever so fast.
No two are the same.
Constantly they're changing, one second one way,
The next second something else.
Floating carelessly, gliding, and even running.
Some may be dense to start then colliding with
another for fullness.
Clouds so puffy, even hiding the moon,
Or perhaps endless blue sky that seems to go on forever.

DID YOU CALL

I thought I heard you call out to me.
I turned around, but did not see, the person I really wanted to be there.
The road was long, blank, and bear.
I turned away and shook my head.
"Could that have been in my mind," I said.
It's possible since you are all ways on my mind.
I'll keep searching and searching until you,
I find.
I'll be looking for you. There will be no stopping.
I may be here or there, even letter dropping.
Trust me, I'll find you. So don't give up on me.
It will take much effort, don't you agree?
Next time I turn and hear that sound,
I'll stop and put a face on whom I'm chasing down.

DO NOT BE MISLED

If you steal, lie, or cheat
Do not be misled, you will be caught in time.
If you live a life of promiscuity
Do not be misled, your lifestyle will follow you.
If you associate with those of questionable habits and morals
Do not be misled, just as milk films a pitcher, their habits will rub off on you.
If you fool yourself by living a double life
Do not be misled, Almighty God sees and will reveal who you truly are from within.
If you give to those of lesser means,
Do not be misled, your Heavenly Father will reward you well.
If you deal with others as you would like to be treated
Do not be misled, others will gravitate to you.
If you speak consoling words to a depressed friend,
Do not be misled, those words could change someone's life.
Whatever you do or whatever you say
Do not be misled.

DON'T TAKE LIFE FOR GRANTED

We can't afford to take things for granted.
In just a matter of seconds, lives can be changed.
This morning when you awakened, did you take for granted your next breath?
To those with respiratory ailments, never can they take breathing for granted.
Perhaps you heard the sound of birds singing so sweetly in the morning.
If the deaf were given that gift of hearing, surely they would never take it for granted.
Maybe first in the morning you look over and greeted your husband, wife, or child.
To those without sight, would they take sight for granted?
Never.
Did you take for granted this morning being able to say,
"Good Morning?"
To those that are mute, would not waste taking speech for granted.
And of course, when you arose today, did you stand right up and stretch nice and tall?
Arthritic limbs and joints never get to take standing and moving for granted.
The gift of smell, how wonderful.
Just ponder what it would be like not smelling a delicious dish.
Be grateful for whatever you are able to accomplish.
Never, no never, take living and loving for granted.

DON'T CRY FOR ME

I am not rich by your measures
Though endowed in me is a priceless treasure
No money can buy what has been given to me
A release from man's bondage, I've been set free

Crime, hatred on the increase and yet I can smile
With the satisfaction that these things are momentary all the while
I awaken to a lovely day even if it rains
Never will I allow this system to place me in it's chains

So much beauty we take for granted every day
Our ability to see or even to listening to the things we say
Yet, these are things deprived to some
Like those that are deaf and dumb

I am loved so dearly by my mate
He's always there for me, I don't have to wait
I have a measure of health to do my daily task
I can sit in the sunlight and bask

I don't have loads of money
But I am rich with the love of my "honey"
He and Jehovah God provide well for me
I hope everyone can see

So please don't cry for me
For I am rich and free
In more ways than one
I am very happy when all is said and done

EVERLASTING LOVE

Once in a lifetime or maybe even twice
Finding eternal love makes you pay the price
It's not always easy to find your mate for life
But the final end is glorious as husband and wife

The new world order promises contentment and peace
Enjoy your mate eternally in each others "love feast"
All these enjoyable things shared by two
Makes love grow as Jehovah God intended it to do
Have fun with the mate of your youth
Happiness and satisfaction you'll find if they are in the truth
No time for jeopardizing everlasting love
Pray before hand to your heavenly Father above
Everlasting love, well it's not a mere dream
Together with your loving mate will make you beam
Could there be anything more fulfilling
No not hardly and it's oh so thrilling

Take your time before taking a step so great
If necessary, lean upon Jehovah and wait
It's far too important to Jehovah and YOU
If proper attention is given, your tears will be few

FREEDOM PARK (Charlotte, NC)

A park of so many angles and turns.
Trees of different descriptions and ferns.
Play grounds, sand piles, swings, and sliding boards, a wonderful day
to spend at the park if the time you can afford.
All the foliage awakening after it's winters rest.
New grass and flowers again, growing so that the park looks it's best.
I'm intrigued with the hills, the fountains, and especially the lake.
It is so worth the trip to make.
We looked high and low to find this spot.
I'm enjoying watching parents playing with their tiny tots.
Learn to take advantage of these simple pleasures.
The moments you're here, you know you will treasure.
This park is not small by any measure of the word.
There are ducks, geese, and lots of birds.
And listen, there, their calls I've heard.
The park air filled with birds, and laughter, no longer is it mute.
Trees putting on their bright new suits.
A retired train engine resides here as a landmark.
Such a nice addition to this lovely Freedom Park.
Thank you for taking this journey with me.
Opening up Freedom Park for everyone to see.

FRIENDS

When things go well and you feel so elated,
share the news with someone to whom you may not be related.
Friends we develop through the years.
So many life's events that bring on joys and tears.
From one extreme to another,
they are right there with us and it's no bother.
It always feel so good to be able to share.
With this loving person who deeply cares.
This person is truly a lifelong friend.
They give us assistance through thick and thin.
Long night chats for no reason at all.
Ready and able to catch you when you fall.
Call them up at any point in time.
And, yes, they'll give you their very last dime.
I can remember the excitement of my graduation day,
or just get-togethers to eat or to play.
It is so important to have a true friend.
They'll stick with you to the very end.

FROM AFAR

Beneath a rising evening moon, sits a couple, Micael and Cynthia, on a bench in their garden.
A beautiful garden it is, with a couple of bird baths.

Within their little piece of paradise, is a countless array of flowers.
Roses, daises, and tulips, are there. So delightful to breath.
Dogwood trees of white and pink swaying against the nudge of the wind.
Birds, robins and blue jays, are chirping and swooping.
This beauty only enhances the mood and time for this pair.

Just the two, chatting low, maybe about their days activity or about how wonderful to spend quality time together.
No way one can overlook the look of love they have for each other.
A genuine heartfelt warmth is radiated in their smiles and the gentleness of their embrace.

The years have been kind to them, both.
Of course, like all couples, they had problems and difficulties, too.
However, they weathered the storm.
His hair is silver and eyes still as a new star.
She's lovely, wearing a smile like soft, delicate lace.

Nothing interrupts the pleasantness of quiet moments.
Television shows, radio programs, not even me, their daughter, should infringe on them.
This is time bought from other mundane things, just for themselves, daily.
No wonder they are still so much in love.

Now I reflect on myself.
I can only hope the years will be as kind to my husband and I.
An evening of intimate togetherness that only they control.
For just this moment, though, I find joy in watching them from afar
and learning from their moments of love.

FROM DEEP WITHIN

From deep within my very being I cry out to you.
The pain of heart and the despair of being blue.
You listen, you hear me, and touch my kidneys and my heart.
I come to realize in the scheme of life I also play an important part.
All of the whys, when, where, and how's, I ask.
I take on everything easier, it's not such a task.
Your peace and satisfaction fondles my very soul.
How grand, for anxieties can and does take it's toll.
Holding your hand, I feel an inner strength. I did not know.
Now I have a confidence that does show.
There is nothing I am able to do of my own will.
By his power I could climb any and every hill.
He's always there to help if we give him a chance.
On his side I take a firm stance.
Yes, he is my God and my Father.
I am here to do your will.

GOLDEN YEARS

Nervous hands and trembling voices
In your life you have made many choices
From where will you live to will you have a family or not
Decisions leaving behind lifelong memories may be your lot

Looking back on all those years
How mom and dad could deflect your fears
Remember having those skinned up knees and that broken heart
They were there to help them heal; they did their part

To school and college, no problem was too big
Think back on dad helping you to identify that twig
All the loving care and directions they invested in you
Would shape you and this they knew

Now the days go by so very fast
Quickly today will turn into the past
You're leaving your mark, no matter how small
Likewise, you did not first walk, you had to crawl

Think for a moment on the lives you touch
You have developed friends that love you so much
A good name you have made with them
As I am sure you are prized as a precious gem

Now your hair resembles white snow
You speak in a whisper or sweet and low
Delicate and priceless is your worth
Today you are just as at your birth

It's time for you to enjoy a bit slower pace
Take your time, there's no need to race
You dealt with that in earlier years
Enjoy your teas, strolls, and chats, my dear

GRANDMA'S HOUSE

Here's some candy
Here's some cake
Help yourself
And please don't wait

There's chocolates, peanuts, and caramel too
I know you'll enjoy it
I can promise you

This is a little store just for tots
A special just for them to go
So come on, come on in
Oh, don't be so slow

A place to stop
A place to have fun
You must know
It is strange to none

Where am I
Where can I be
Could I be dreaming
To feel so much glee

There's only one place that I could be
There's just this one places to be so free
Who's that sitting in that rocking chair
Aww, it's my grandma over there

HEAVENLY BODIES - REMIND ME OF YOU

When we are apart and I feel so alone,
I look up at he sun or moon or stars
And ponder on you enjoying these very same heavenly bodies. I love gazing at the stars and watching them twinkle.
It is at that time that I remember that twinkle that I last saw in your eyes.

The sun, so bright, is always there for us.
You have it there, and I have it here.
How exciting that it's the same sun.
When I think of the brilliance the sun gives off, then I think of the brilliance of your smiling disposition.

The moon that lights up the night, we both share.
It's not as bright as the sun, but makes an enormous impact on the earth. The moon reminds me of the little things you say and do for me. How I appreciate your loving and kind demeanor.

Rain refreshes what has become dried from the sun. It invigorates and enlivens what it descends upon. You have had that effect on me. Being in your life is like a warm spring shower that brings my feelings for you to life. Your words of endearment keeps my love for you growing all the more.

The thunder and lightning causes me to reflect on some of my more difficult moments when I run to you for shelter from the storm. You're my hiding place from the turmoil that comes upon me from time to time. You have proven yourself to be my haven and my "home."

Air and water are two of life's necessities.
Without them we can not function.
Now that you are a part of my life, you are so necessary because of our love. I am dependent on you as I am dependent on water and air to live. Water, so smooth and soothing to the soul. Air that's crisp and so sweet to breath, seems to rejuvenate you as I am when you're with me.

These heavenly bodies, enjoyed by both of us in different locations, helps us to feel closer though many miles a part. The sun, moon, stars, and even the air I breathe, reminds me of you. I sit quietly in my room meditating on how fulfilling it is to love you.

I AM A REFLECTION OF LOVE

The love I have is reinforced by the love shown to me.
I am the product of so much love.
My parents loved each other and their children.
It had to be love to have had ten babies.
Memories of family dinners and outings and all filled with love.

The love I give to you is a tenderness that I cherished that others
Bestow upon me.
A smile comes to me when I think of situations and enjoyable
Moments.
Watching shinning eyes of little ones gleaming just by giving them
A bit of time and energy.
Scooping a baby up in my arms and receiving a strong hug and big
Smile contributes to the love I have.

Having, too, someone who loves me dearly, knowing that his love is
Genuine and so sincere.
No words conveys our love for each other through good times and
bad.
Another measure of love that I consume and thrive on.
Then there's the love from my heavenly Father.
I never have to worry of his love and support.
He's proven to be my tower of strength. Even if friend and family
turn
Their backs on me, my heavenly Father would be there to give me
the
Love I need.

So again, the love I have is merely a reflection of the love that has
been
Bestowed on me by my loved ones.

I GIVE TO YOU

I wish I could give you a perfect day, but perfection is not mine to give.
I give you my peace and happiness.
I wanted to give you something but did not know what.
So I looked deep down inside myself and here is what I have got:

I give you my SHOULDER when you need support.
I give to you my HAND when you need me close.
I give to you my EARS to listen to you when you need to talk.
I give to you my LIPS to say words that will up build and not tear down.
Above all that I give you, I give you MY LOVE.

May it keep you warm knowing that I care so much.
May your day be filled with all the brightness that the sun can muster and all the blue sky the heavens can unveil.

I LOVE CALLING NORTH CAROLINA HOME

Some may say, they "love calling NC home."
I must admit by this coast, I have been groomed.
It is situated right on the Atlantic Ocean.
Settling here was no mere notion.

I've traveled to places both here and there.
The Carolinas and I are the perfect pair.
Ocean, beaches on the coast, and mountains
To the West,
Lovely as they are, I love the East Coast best.

Being away from here, I'd be a fish out of water.
If you're looking for a place to stay, try eastern
NC for starters.
You won't be sorry, I can promise you.
There are many attractions and things to do.

Coastal Carolina, perfect to raise a family or retire.
Wonderful real estate, you'll surely become a buyer.
Houses of every description to choose from.
An inviting area just beckoning you to "come."

Our visitors here, can't wait to come back.
The people, the activities, nothing does the
East Coast lack.
Now check with your travel agent and set a date.
It's right here in eastern NC, don't make us wait.

I NEVER

I never dreamed of meeting someone like you that could be so much like me.
Your personality, your sense of humor, and the your calm and mild spirit.

I never thought of finding you. You who complete me in every way, spiritually, emotionally, intellectually, and physically.
I always hoped that my soul mate was out there. Only Jehovah God knew who he was and where he was.
That person was you. I am so grateful that you were led to me.

I never felt feelings like I feel now.
The feelings of being loved so completely.
You make me feel beautiful and so wanted.
It is so comforting to have a lover that just feels so right in my life.

I never loved someone so much, being engulfed in their love. How wonderful to find a love so matchless and limitless.
I love you more that life. Never could I or would I love someone more than you.

AN INSPIRATIONAL THOUGHT

This is the first day of the rest of your life.
Every day is full of new beginnings and new adventures.
There are so many places to discover, and experiences to enjoy.
Always do your best today, for tomorrow belongs to none of us.
Make your time count and be an asset to society.
The moment you just had will never come again.
How was it spent? Was it beneficial or frivolously squandered on empty pursuits?
Make every moment, every hour, and every day meaningful.
Do not waste it, for it will come around only once in your lifetime.

I SHARE YOUR LOSS

A heart that is broken by pain and grief, makes life unbearable at times.
To lose a loved one to death can make one feel helpless and scared.
Death has been called "an enemy."
It does rob us of those we truly love.
Sharing lives with our families is the way it's suppose to be.
Take a moment to think about your late loved one.
Give some time to reflect on all the good things that you have done together.
Remember that outing at the beach, or a nice long drive with the family?
Now can you hear the laughter and then see the smiles on everyone?
Those were very good times.
Nothing and no one can take those moments from you.
Precious, and priceless are words depicting the great memories.
Keep them burning bright in your heart and mind.
When these over powering feelings of despair gets you down, think on the good times.
Re-envision him or her and those happier times.
Time will help to lessen the pain, but it will never erase the memories left behind.
Allow yourself to grieve, that is a part of the healing.
Maintain a positive attitude and look to the future with courage.
Times WILL get better.

IN THE STILLNESS OF THE NIGHT

In the stillness of the night,
I search for you and you aren't there.
But left behind are the wonderful feelings and emotions that we
shared when we were together last.

In the stillness of the night,
I silently recall the splendor of your love, the gleam in your eye, and
the softness of your touch. I also recall the smell of your aftershave
and the sweetness of your cologne.

In the stillness of the night,
I close my eyes and dream of you. Dreams in vivid colors and
shapes so perfect and relaxing to the mind. Dreams so real that
when I awake I feel refreshed as if you were with me and we shared a
holiday together.

In the stillness of the night,
I'm left alone with my thoughts of you, your laughter, your smile,
and your witty sense of humor. It's my thinking of you that keeps
me enduring until the time when next we meet.

In the stillness of the night,
I'm waiting for our returning to each other with open arms. Our
time has arrived to be with one another, now and forever more.
The stillness of the night,
Will no more be.
You are here and the night is no longer still, but filled with laughter,
life, and love.

INTERNAL HEALING BY THE SPRING

Have you ever had a day you just felt out of sorts?
But you opened your eyes to a lovely Spring day?
The sky is blue, and the air is so gentle.
The dogwood trees are beginning to blossom.
You now have the assurance that warmer weather is on it's way.
Now that you are in the sun, it seems to rejuvenate you.
That dreary feeling you had is wearing away.
Listen to the call of the birds in the morning.
How lovely.
And look, there. Do you see that?
It's our friendly woodpecker again this year.
There's something special about that one tree he seems to love.
He always return to peck that tree most.
It's a new year and a new Spring.
Hearing the sounds, seeing the sights, and absorbing the warmth of the sun has a way of brightening your day.
Being engulfed in natural surroundings is sohealthy for us.
At least I find it that way for me.
Although I arose not feeling my best,
As the morning goes on, those bad feelings regress.

IT IS NO ONES FAULT

It is no ones fault, just remember that.
We make mistakes and err many times.

Sometimes, things are said and feelings are hurt.
One cannot wear ones feelings on their shoulders.

The hardest thing to say at times is, "I'm Sorry."
However, they are two small words but can repair the deepest of cuts.
It has a way of mending when all else fails.

Nothing ever goes too far that cannot be rectified.

Be humble enough not to think too much of yourself.
You are human and so am I.
It is just a misunderstanding.

Forgive me.

KATRINA'S BLOW - CONTINUES

It has been several years since hurricane Katrina hit.
Still there are houses deplorable and unfit.
Homes ripped apart or even condemned.
Their plight is so much worse in the end.
These people still trying to get their lives back in some order.
Their sanity still hangs near insanity's border.
So many loss everything they had.
Now they need more loving help so very bad.
Even the little trailers where they were allowed to use,
Because of asbestos they will also them loose.
I can imagine a feeling of "where can I turn."
We wish we could help and our hearts yearn.
Some have been able to regroup and restart.
Yet they exhaust themselves to do their part.
Keep these in our thoughts and our prayers.
We watched this on TV as it unfolded and aired.
Having to live in bad situations will carry scars that will always be.
Thinking on them or even may times while trying to sleep, they'll
recollect and in their minds eyes they will see.
Many children left up to the mercy of man.
Around each and everyone of them, we need to band.
So for all these years they still are in need of care.
Their plight was truly very unfair.
They may survive if we all pitch in.
After all, they are our brothers, sisters, companions, and friends.

KATRINA'S BLOW

Faces showing complete despair
The smell of sewage and death in the air
Deplorable conditions where no one should have to live
Scenes of this in their minds, they'll constantly relive
Merely surviving on NO shelter, NO water, and NO food
Surely there was no choice than to darken the mood
Trying to hold on to loved ones so dear
Being ripped away from each other, heightens their fears
"Take my hand, my child," or "hold on my wife"
A war from within, so much strife
Loosing one's family in a stampeding crowd
Your mind plays tricks and your thoughts are shroud
Waters and debris rising ever so sure
No more drinking water so pure
Not even a clean, dry spot to lay their head
Sick people, hurt people, and over there, the dead
Minutes, hours, and days go by
The voices, oh the voices, babies cry
Immediate care and attention is what these need
Who would have thought this is where hurricane Katrina could lead
Children had to grow up fast
They are usually the ones thought of last
We try to shield them from pain
Sometimes parents break under the strain
Now that recovery effort have begun
It's truly a nightmare, there is NO fun
These people may never get their lives back in order
Their mental state weighs close to insanity's border

Better days will soon come
Due to heartache and pain, people are numb
Fellow-feeling and kindness all must learn
Wanting to do more, inside we yearn
Giving of ourselves, our times, and our money
This is the beginning of a long hard journey
May it help to know that others care
We desire one and all to be treated fair.

LAUGH OUT LOUD

Some of us take ourselves so serious.
We are starched, stiff, and never gregarious.
Laughter actually has a healing force.
To be happy or sad is our choice.
We are not perfect so we make mistakes.
In deed or word, even promises we brake.
Lighten up, for laughter tickles the soul.
People warm up to us, if we do not appear cold.
A hearty laugh releases stress.
It changes our attitude from dull to fresh.
Many of us can not laugh, we giggle instead.
Think of something funny and first laugh upon your bed.
Have you ever had a friend that brought you to laughter just by looking at their face?
I remember those moments and ever so often, them I retrace.
Laughter from the stomach is great for the heart.
When it comes from deep within it plays an important part.
So learn from a child just how to laugh. a, belly giggler, teary eyed, out of control laugh.

LET'S TAKE A WALK

Let's take a walk, hand in hand.
Across the meadows, through the hills and over land,
From the highest peak to even beaches sand.

Let's take a walk and converse on the way, about life, love, and all the things
Jehovah God has to say.
From obeying Him never may we stray.
Keeping our eyes focused on the kingdom hope, come what may.

Let's take a walk just to clear our heads,
Of all the negative things people have said.
Things that at times makes us happy or afraid.

Let's take a walk for our love
Appreciating Jehovah's beauty from above.
Always know that it's you, I'll always love.
No one there to push or shove let's take a walk . . .

LET'S TAKE A MENTAL JOURNEY

Paint a picture in your mind.
Choose your favorite season of the year.
My favorite season is Fall or Autumn.
Let me share my picture with you.
A nice cool breeze that makes the trees bow and dip.
Trees of so many colors, yellow, green, and red.
I've not seen trees so colorful in a long time.
Lawn's all carpeted with leaves.
There's no wonder why children love romping in them.
I don't know how people in NY deal with no trees around their homes.
There are not many flowers left to gaze upon, but the trees make up where the flowers leave off.
Take a drive to the beach.
Don't forget to wear something warm.
The ocean is beautiful and the waves, too.
There are still people walking on the shoreline.
Sit for a bit to clear your mind.
As the evening wears on, there is a gorgeous sunset.
Tells us it is time to pack up and head home.
Now it is time to stop daydreaming.
It is back to reality and I am totally relaxed.

THE LITTLE GIRL WITH THE BIG BROWN EYES

Standing here is a sweet little girl with big brown eyes.
A smile of sunshine, shielding a heart that cries.

Although she's very fragile, when she's helping others, she's so strong.
We may never know exactly what in her life went wrong.

I've heard that death claimed both her mom and her dad.
If that be the case, there's no wonder she's many times, sad.

Just think no one to run to when she is hurting or in pain.
She was a part of a family, but now she feels like links were taken from her chain.

That has to be traumatic for any child.
Yet she has a sweet demeanor and is so very mild.

A day goes by and so does years,
The smile is still there and the eyes are bright.
But there have been tears.

I guess it is to be expected, for she would feel that loss from time to time.
One can only hope that her friends can help her above this climb.

She does try to take everything in stride.
Her parents will forever in her heart reside.
Now though it is her day. Her wedding day.
It is going to be lovely, come what may.

Finally she has a family of her own.
If only her parents could see her and how she's grown.
A husband she has taking to be right by her side.
Comforting to know, in him she can confide.

She loves him, and he's gained her trust.
They love each other and their happiness is a must.
Never could I forget this little girl with the big brown eyes.
Stronger now than ever, are her family ties.

MEMORIES

We've been endowed with the gift of memory.
Some are good and others are not as pleasant.
It is important to keep things in the right perspective.
Life is full of pleasantries if we stop and smell the roses.
Every day we arise to a new day.
To spend time with our loved ones.
And all the while memories are being made.
They are not always the big things we remember.
Do you recall looking toward your mate from across the room?
There was the warmest smile and twinkle in their eyes.
What about the walks you took, just holding your child's hand?
Was that not comforting and pleasant?
Each intricate action we make forms a memory of some sort.
Now there are those memories of pain and grief.
Do not despair, you will get through it.
Some one gets sick, someone gets hurt, and we loose them to death.
That's where this wonderful gift of memories comes into play.
Although we aren't able to interact with them every day,
We will forever keep memories of them alive.
Those are good, yet more difficult times try not to ponder on
More than is necessary.
The happy memories keep to the fore.
Play them up in your mind and heart.
They give you a warm cozy feeling deep down inside.

MY BEST FRIEND

My best friend always listens when I need him.
Without any doubt, he is truly a gem.
If I am not feeling my best, he's right there.
He shows by his actions that he does sincerely care.
I can look across the room and catch his eye,
Then I know the answers to all the whys?
Why do I love him and he loves me?
Why does he make me feel so free?
Why has he invested all this time and effort in us?

Implicitly in him, I've placed my trust.
My best friend and I enjoy spending time together.
It matters not what ever the weather.

MY HUSBAND - MY LOVE

(Dedicated to my husband Micael)

When I think of you
I think of sharing our lives
I think of contentment
I think of togetherness
I see your tenderness
I see your kindness
In you I see my paradise

When I close my eyes
I ponder on your smile
I ponder on your eyes
I ponder on your face
I hear your voice
I hear your laughter
I hear the ocean from afar

When I think of you
When I close my eyes
I feel how close we truly are
I feel the love we share
I feel the warmth of your presence
I feel the security of you
My Husband - My Love

"MY LITTLE SISTER"

(Dedicated to Kirstie)

I remember you as a little girl.
With beaming eyes and a smile that could melt a heart.
You were so warm and adorable.
Did I mention your eyes were like new stars?

I remember playing with your tiny little fingers.
You would hold on so tight to my hand.
Taking big baby steps just learning to walk.
You were independent ever at that early age.

I remember you singing to your Nana on the phone,
Realizing then just how sweet you truly were.
It didn't take much to keep you happy.
You had a life uncluttered with material things.

You continued to grow into a lovely young lady.
Word's doesn't express how proud I am of you.
Reflecting on you, brings me much pleasure.
You truly are a lovely young woman and I love you.

MY SISTER --- MY JOY

(Dedicated to Eva)

I look up to you as my big sister.
As a little girl, I wanted to be just like you.
You always had a kind spirit.
You were always willing to go the extra mile for someone.

I admired your strength.
Your laughter is infectious.
I have learned much from you.
I will forever be observing and learning.

Remember the long talks on the phone we'd have?
Weekends of long chats and shopping trips for the day, remember them?
I enjoyed just the thought of being with you, my big sister.
Well I can not forget the many vacations we've shared, from Disney World to Bermuda.

Those times are wonderful memories.
They were moments of sheer joy.
So much love I have for you, my sister.
Just keep on keeping on.
May we continue growing and making memories. Together.

PARADISE INDEED

Allow me, please, to tell you about my dream.
Is it true? What does it all mean?
I see fields of the best grain ever.
No shortage of food. Never. No Never.

Trees and grass luscious and green.
There's no garbage or trash, just completely clean.
It's a lovely place, I wish you were here.
I'll try to paint you a picture that's vivid and clear.

Children and animals playing and having fun.
Everywhere there's happiness, no sadness. None.
People gladly handling all their chores.
Beautiful waters and warm sand on the sea shores.

No one seems to be tired or sick.
In my mind things are beginning to click.
Just look. There! None there are old.
They are youthful, vibrant, strong, and bold.

This is a wonderful time to live.
Young and old, both alike, ready to give.
A paradise is what this certainly has to be.
Absolutely, there's a feeling of being set free.

REFLECTIONS

Have you ever felt an ocean breeze, or seen the wind blowing through trees?
Have you ever watched birds in flight, gliding and reaching enormous heights?

Have you ever felt a cool summer rain, or listened to the whistle of a moving train?
Have you ever watched children at play, or stopped to listen to what they have to say?

Have you ever seen shapes in a cloud, or heard a thundercloud, so loud?
Have you ever made ripples in a pond, or played with a puppy and seen him respond?

Have you ever pondered the vastness of space, or the features of a loved ones face?
Have you ever felt true peace of mind, or thought what it's like to be color-blind?

If you reflect on life's tiny experience, then you will appreciate God's magnificence.
Happy we are with these little things.
Memories of these we tightly cling.

REFRESHED BY A DREAM

I have been told that dreams are healthy.
You can enjoy them whether poor or wealthy.
They appear to be serious, funny, romantic, or even bad.
Some relaxes us and some makes us feel sad.
The ones we remember most are those we relate to.
We dream in colors and different hues.
In our mind, pictures are painted so real.
We smell flowers and things that we can feel.
Have you ever had a dream so relaxing you feel refreshed when you awaken?
It was just a dream, don't be mistaken.
Dreams release a lot of pinned up emotions.
We dream about loved ones as a notion.
Remember that special evening with your loving mate?
Late at night you dream and relive that date.
Places, faces, smells, and sounds come to mind.
Old friends forgotten, in a dream, suddenly again we find.
So refreshing it is to close your eyes and daydream of a garden of peace and serenity.
No guns, no fighting, no hate in this vicinity.
So next time when you go to sleep,
Develop memories that you'll always keep.

I AM REMEMBERING YOU WITH LOVE

I remember the smell of your cologne
Silently I think of you, you are here, and I am not alone
I remember how your laughter lights up a room
Thoughts of you makes my spirit soar and loom
I remember the gentleness of your touch
That is just one of the things that I truly miss so much
I remember the comfort and security of being in your arms
My very being, from deep within, feels warm
I remember the softness of your kiss
Now that is one of the things also that I miss
Yes, I am remembering just now your kiss
Of course I cannot forget that first moment of bliss
I remember sitting close to you and you holding my hand
Knowing that I am yours and the flames of love are fanned
Oh yes, I am remembering that look in your eye when you need me
I know you; I do, and understand your unspoken plea
I am remembering the feeling of your body against mine
My body, soul, and spirit, toward you, I am inclined
I remember the first time that you said, "I love you"
It was at that point that I knew your love for me was so true
I remember a passionate glance from afar
Or that quick glance while driving in our car
I remember that peaceful look on your face when you sleep
Or the way you, so lovingly, care for me when I weep
I remember the day you asked me to be your bride
You never knew, with such happiness, I cried
I remember so many things that is only YOU
We'll have a lifetime of remembrances when we are no longer two

RESURRECTION HOPE

The resurrection hope means so much to me.
Family, friends, and dear ones returning for all to see.
Jesus gave us hope with those he brought back from the dead.
Some were so very sick upon their beds.
Loved ones returning from what seems a brief sleep.
Being so happy can cause us to weep.
It is a wonderful gift of life Jehovah God has given us.
With all this evidence from the Bible, we have reason in him to place our trust.
In a little while, the resurrection will start.
I want to be there, to do my part.
There are so many I can't wait to see.
I close my eyes, Jehovah hear my plea.
I can't wait to welcome back my dad and mom.
We know from where she and the others come from.
We'll have a resurrection party for those being brought back.
Physically and mentally, nothing will they lack.
These ones will have to trained of Jehovah's ways.
Rightly so, for they will be under his direction all of their days.
People who don't know him will have to be taught.
Some will be surprised, still others, distraught.
In due time all will get to love him as we do.
And also to be peace promoters too.
Everlasting life has been placed in our hearts.
Love, humility, kindness, and mercy from his word he imparts.
Such a blessed time it then will be.
No more pain, no more sickness, only true peace and security.

RUNNING FREE

There is a simple joy in a child chasing birds.
How innocent, yet intriguing when shared by two generations.
A mother and her daughter running, playing, and laughing together.
On a beach with the rising sun, taking part in tailoring the growth
of youth.
As the day grows evermore, a happiness, an elation that can't be
replaced by money.
It can not be bought with things.
A sincere true inner peace, they share.
Such a profound sweetness these two are engulfed in.
I find myself giving way to tears just watching
The interchange of moments, or a loving touch.
We take so much for granted.
We complicate things by over analyzing and looking for motives.
Take a moment to stop, relax, and watch children running free.

SENIOR MOMENTS IN TIME

Feeble knees and trembling voices
Tells forth a history of many choices
What kind of job, or where shall I stay
Days of thoughts and at night I pray

Changes, oh my, the changes I've seen
Myself from vibrant to upon this cane I lean
I use to walk, jog, run and race
Now my steps are short and a much slower pace

My eyes aren't as bright as they use to be
I don't see as well as I use to see
Everything changes as years go by
I'm more sentimental and easier to cry

Those little members in my mouth that helped me to eat
I find it more difficult to chew meat
Apples, corn, hard candy, and such
A problem I have with eating, though
I enjoyed them so much

My hearing isn't as crisp as it use to be
Yet still I love to hear children laughing free
Simple things now, I really enjoy
I get excited like a child with a new toy

It seems I don't need eight hours of sleep
From a chair I rise slowly, never do I leap
New things I can't remember like I do the old
And oh my goodness, the tells that I've told

To say all of this, the years have been kind
Making the most of my time I've been inclined
Yet still, I thank God for every new day
So I rise in the morning and get on my way.

SIMPLE PLEASURES

Please don't underestimate the sheer joy that comes from
Childlike simplicity. Have you ever noticed the smile on a child's
face when he is eating his favorite ice cream cone? Or the delight
of a little boy walking in the rain especially when there's a puddle
along the way?
Or maybe see the gleam in their eye when
Nana or Papa is around?
Much can be learned from observing a child.
Take the time to feel the sun on your skin. Or perhaps rise early in
the morning and listen to the birds greeting a new day.
Instead of running to get out of the rain, take yourself a walk in the
rain.
Do you feel invigorated?
Simple little pleasures can sometimes bring peace of mind.
Just remember every day has it's own anxieties, so take the time to
relax and breathe.
That's a perfect way to de-stress.

SOMEBODY LOVES YOU

Somebody loves you, deeply from the heart.
In her life, you play a major part.
Somebody loves you, and needs you in the warmest way.
Having you close to love, may you forever stay.
Somebody loves you, and wants you this to know.
She loves you, she admits, and don't mind   saying so.
Somebody loves you, and now I wonder who it could be?
Well let me take a moment.
Hmmmm can't you see...?
Somebody loves you.
Oh yes, that's what she said.
She also said upon her heart, only you do tread.
Somebody loves you, who could it ever be?
Well, look no further.
That Somebody is ME!!!

SOMEWHERE IN TIME, I WILL FIND MY HAPPINESS

At different times in our lives we suffer stress.
Heartache, disappointments, and sadness makes us feel depressed.
Oh how these feelings make our hearts regress.
Yet how we respond under a loved ones gentle caress.

When feeling forlorn and just out of touch,
We don't feel or realize we're loved so much.
Lets take these bad feelings and lock them in a hutch.
So wonderful when our hearts and souls are touched.

Pressures and anxieties are always there.
It does help to know that someone cares.
Our pains and hurts, they try to bear.
This mental stress is assuredly not fair.

To know we have family and friends by our side,
Makes dealing with depression nothing to hide.
We share with them our feelings and in them confide.
It's hard for us to open our hearts wide.

But somewhere in time, I'll find my happiness.
I will look deep within myself to find my peacefulness.
Never shall I give up my stick-to-itiveness,
Because it means my everlasting happiness.

STANDING BY MY FRIEND

When you think you are weak,
I will help you be strong.
When you feel you can't go on,
I'll be there to cheer you on to the finish.
When your "spirit" has been crushed,
I'll be by your side to help you mend it.
When you can't see the light at the end of the tunnel,
I'll light up your darkness.
When you are nervous, uneasy, and can not rest,
I'll give you my peace to relax your mind and heart.
When you are forlorn and feel so alone, you will have my hand to
hold giving you assurance that I'll always be here.
When you feel you can't keep your head above water,
I'll give you a boost to raise you up.
When your sunny skies began to turn dark,
I'll be there to roll that dark cloud back.
When you are vexed,
I'll be there to say "everything will be alright."
When you are perplexed,
I'll be by your side to help you find your way clear.
When the walls began to close in on you,
I'll be there to push them back.
When you feel you can't,
When you think you can't,
I'll be with you to help you accomplish your goal.

STRANGERS OF THE NIGHT

We are two strangers passing in the night. Neither one of us knowing that the person standing by us would change our lives forever. Not even thinking when we paused or caught each others eye.

Under a moonlit sky we begin to speak. Exchanging names, hopes, and dreams. Conversing softly and unhurriedly we tap into each others mind and heart. Who really is this person? Could this be the person I've waited for so long, and NOW is so close to me?

The night wears on and on, but we don't mind. Actually, we've lost track of time. The tiredness of the day has passed by and I feel rejuvenated, like I've had a peaceful sleep and have awaken feeling refreshed. When truly I am awake.

We exchanged addresses in hopes of meeting this passing person again. Soon. No longer can I call him a stranger. Such a pleasant evening. I did not want it to end.

Well that was many years ago this month. The letters never stopped, the calls never stopped, the visits never stopped.
Memories were constantly being made. I still remember that night so fondly. That was the night that changed my life.

Thank you for all these years of love, compassion, affection, tenderness, and companionship. On this starlit night, I stop and close my eyes. I think of you and feel your presence. I open my eyes and you are with me, now, by my side. I turn to you, knowing you knew how I must be feeling. You have those feelings too and so deliberately tell me in my ear.

As first we met, we stand in silence. Arm in arm, reliving those memories. These times I put in my treasured storehouse of memories gold. When we are not together, I relive one of those moments with you, if only in my mind.

Forever keep the stars twinkling and our light burning bright in both our hearts. Within the quietest of strangers, lies a gem waiting to be brought to life. When all is said and done, I loved you then, now, and forevermore.

SUNSETS

There can be nothing lovelier than the sight of a setting sun.
So beautiful. So serene. So calming.
Imagine a sunset over an ocean or beach.
On a windy day the sky turns a fabulous shade of lavender.

There are birds soaring in the heaven that are enjoying the sunsets, too.
However, they don't appreciate the warm colors and hues changing tenses.
They look so majestic flying free and easy.

Listen to the waves crashing against the shore, rushing across the sunset painted sand.
At times you can feel the spray of the waves on your face.
So peaceful.
So lovely.

The sunset continues changing as we speak.
It will not be complete until it is covered over by the clouds.
Little by little it's lovely shades are fading.
So inspiring it is to gaze at it's beauty.
We don't control it. We can't buy it.
It is a precious gift.
Take an evening and reflect on the setting sun.
It will give your spirit a lift.

TABLES DO TURN

(Dedicated to the families touched by Alzheimer's Disease)

Strange how times change.
I looked to you to heal my hurts and to wipe away those frustrating tears.
Learning to button a shirt or to tie my shoes are huge accomplishments for me.
You taught me how to comb my hair and the task of going to the bathroom.
I knew I was a big girl when I was able to do all those things all by myself.
Through it all, you were right there, encouraging me through trial and error.
It was not easy, I'm sure of that.
But now the table has turned.
Now I am the one you look up to to heal the hurts and all the pains.
Buttoning shirts and tying shoes are a chore for you, but you keep on trying.
It is I now who comb and brush your hair.
I recall reminding you to brush your teeth before going to bed.
Never would I complain, for it is not easy by any means.
As it was not easy for you when I was there.
You gave me the courage to keep trying and I intend to do the same.
The table has turned, but it's ok, I love you now as much as you loved me then.
You are my mother and now I am your "mother."
I am your child, yet now you are my "child."
I accept this challenge graciously.

THANKS FOR THE COLORS

When I think on your loving me,
I think of a box of crayons.

YELLOW - for the sunshine you bring me.

RED - for the fire and passion you have brought me.

GREEN - for the growth we have made together.

BROWN - for the earthiness and foundation you have brought to our family.

BLUE - for the blue days we have, but having you right beside me.

ORANGE - for the spice of sharing your culture and your life.

BLACK - for elegance never morbidity.

Our life is full of colors and hues.
Thank you for adding such crisp colors to my life.

THANKS FOR YOUR TIME

Seconds, minutes, and hours go by, seldom do we think of those that pass our way.
Maybe a soft voice or a coarse "Hello" yet that voice belonged to someone who recognized YOU.

We do not pay attention, at times, to how many touch our lives daily.
What about that fellow worker that you feel is a pest?
Did you give any thought that this person cares about YOU and want to wish you well?

What about that gentleman that is ALWAYS there to open that door for you?
We're in so much of a rush, we don't think twice to say "Thank you".
And yet he is always there to lend a hand.
He doesn't HAVE to do it, but he WANTS to do it.

And remember seeing your boss peeking in your area?
And remember you were angered because he was there?
Could it be that your boss enjoys seeing YOUR smile?
Could it be that your boss feels at peace in your space?

And oh my, what about the question your husband asked when you came home from work?
"Honey, what is for dinner?"
Think about it, obviously he loves the way YOU cook.
He'd prefer YOUR cooking over his favorite restaurant.

Negativity is what we think of first.
However, we should be positive and look for the good in things.
Never forget those ones that we touch .
Cherish the minute, hours, days, and weeks that you have together.
Just say, "Thank you for your time and energy in my behalf".

THE BEE AND THE BEE-MAN

"His labor is a chant
His idleness a tune;
Oh, for a bee's experience,
Of clovers and of noon."

These words so true of the hard working bee
But is also true of my husband, Micael V.
Bees, bees, and more bees. You see he truly loves
Working with them.
This is his job, not just a passing whim.

Listening to how he extracts the honey.
It's so interesting, we don't even have to talk about the money.
Time and patience is needed when working with hives.
Attention and endurance will help them thrive.

I had no idea the variety of bees there are.
I do remember, as a little girl, catching bees in a jar.
They are attentive to the queens needs.
Mending the hives and nourishment for her to feed.

Colors of black and yellow, so bright.
Interesting when they're in flight.
We learn so much from these little creatures.
Study them and their many features.

After investigating them, I'm not as afraid of them as I use to be.
In their presence, I'm okay, no worry.
I look at them now for the beauty they carry.
However, if a swarm I see, I will not tarry.

I'll leave them to my husband, the Bee man.
He knows how to handle them and I know he can.
Whether a lot of them or only a few,
He gives them all the respect that's due.

It has been said, "His feet are shod with gauze.
His helmet is of gold
His breast, a single onyx with chrysoprase, in laid."

THE DEATH OF MY DAD

I remember that day, Monday, March 26
Over 30 years ago.
That was a day my heart hurt so.
Forever will I recall the sight of my brother
Bringing my father in our house in his arms.
He was semi-conscious and it caused great alarm.
My mother holding him gently, pulling off his coat.
Watching this, I felt so light headed as being afloat.
Being an avid Bible student, I grabbed my Bible
And began to read.
Happier passages I started to indulge in and feed.
Verses like Rev. 21:3,4 where death will be
Swallowed up forever.
Reflecting on the promise of no more sickness
And death ever, no never.
Strength and inner peace of mind, I found
Although my dad laid there sick.
It seemed so long the ambulance in coming as
The clock ticked.
Fright, pain, and distress, I saw in my mothers
Eyes.
I knew nothing I could say could quiet her cries.
The ambulance finally got to take my daddy away.
Now that my mom is gone and we are so little, who
With us, will stay?
Neighbors and relatives came forward to care for us.
All of this happened so fast, everything was a rush.
It was found that he had a cerebral hemorrhage of
Of the brain.

He was unconscious and was said to feel no pain.
Hard it was going through those next few
Days.
I didn't know if I was going or coming. I felt as if I
Were in a maze.
On Wednesday, March 28th, while at school,
We received the call.
My daddy didn't make it, he had taken
Death's fall.
You see, I remember it just as yesterday.
I am the youngest of several children that
Had to go on, by the way.
So painful and hard it has been at times.
Often, I felt restrained at expressing myself
Like a mime.
For all these years we've been trying to cope.
The Bible constantly gives comfort and
Forever hope.

THE HUMAN FLOWER GARDEN

How wonderful to look at this sea of humanity
Enjoy it, don't be bothered by all this racial insanity
All different colors, sizes, and shades
With time, negativity toward others will fade

Faces slender, oval, square, and round
Dozens of lovely eye colors are found
Green, blue, brown, hazel, and even gray
They can be spell-binding, needless to say

My mind drifts off to a breath-taking field of flowers
So many types, and styles, some low and others tower
Intrigued by distinguishing names to identify them
Whatever the sort, they are truly a gem

Just as flowers need basic things to grow
Humankind, all of us, need basic things to grow and glow
Never loose our simplicity of life
It could lead to heartache and strife

Take a day at the beach or in a park and just observe
Do it. Go on. Get up your nerve
Allow your appreciation for your fellowman to mount
You'll have so many inspiring thoughts, it will be hard to count.

THE RAIN

Seems everyone is racing to get out of the rain
Yet it refreshes things as sleep keeps one from feeling drained
There is beauty in a rainy day
Think of how lovely flowers and trees are in May

How wonderful the smell of flowers so sweet
Things parched and dry are in for a treat
Rain keeps the grass oh so green
Lawn so attractive when they are nice and clean

I am intrigued with the sound of rain
Sometimes it is light other times it sounds like a train
Umbrellas, jackets, are finished off with a hat
No covering to worry about for your dog or cat

Beauty is in everything if you allow yourself to see
Release that child inside of you and set yourself free
Enjoy the elements that keeps things fresh and new
It is just the same with heavy dew

THE WINDS EFFECT

It has been said, ""Who has seen the wind?
Neither you nor I.
But when the leaves bow down their heads, the wind is passing by.""

Intriguing. You can not see the wind, but we can see its effect on things. Take for instance, a leaf. Any leaf. It breaks from a vine, on a branch, on a tree; the wind blows under it, over it, and around it. Soaring, at times miles away, this one lone leaf.

Awesome. You can not grasp the wind, yet you can feel its presence on your skin. Standing on a hill, like my favorite one in Wales. The wind may be blowing in your face, and you sense the presence of it. The wind could even blow your eyelids closed.

Incredible. You can not taste the wind. However, if you were to stick out your tongue on a wind blown day, the coolness of the wind will be left behind to remind you that its there.

Oh so fascinating. You can not touch the wind. None the less, you can hear the wind. Just like the calm winds on a Spring day can be heard. Also the extra strong winds of a hurricane or North-east wind. It may be strong enough to uproot trees or even demolish a house.

Inanimate it is, but how diversified it is. Life would not be the same without it.
Yes it has been said, "Who has seen the wind?
Neither I nor you.
But when the leaves hang golden, the wind is passing through."

THE WONDERS OF NATURE

Nothing can compare to the beauty of nature.
Watching birds in flight, brings us much pleasure.
The softness of a cloud, nothing can measure.
These simple things you should treasure.

Enjoy the serenity of a moonlit night,
Or the heavens full of stars so bright.
Gazing as a little boy flies his kite,
Tugging against the wind with all his might.

Try listening to the wind blowing through a tree.
See it's branches take a bow as if to agree.
Just sitting on the beach in a summer breeze,
It's so much fun these moments we seize.

We are blessed to have a Father who is so very wise.
The ingenuity reflected in how a hummingbird flies.
Prepared for us is everlasting life as a prize.
To every man who, toward God, really tries.

THEY ARE A GIFT - THE FEMININE ONE

Some men have a distorted view of women.
They are not a piece of property like the family car.
She is soft and special.
Imperative it is for men and husbands to recognize her intricate make up.
Do you make it your business to break her spirit and to beat her down?
Do you look at her as a pick-up lady, just to clean and pick up behind you?
If you do, you're missing out on a treasure.
NO longer are you looking at her as the feminine one.
She's now become your possession to wipe you feet on.
This will lead to trouble.
Maybe she's gained some weight, are you going to abuse her because she's not like the models you watch on television?
No longer are you cherishing her, instead, you are crushing her spirit.
If you do that, it takes so much to help her regain her self worth and disposition.
When you forever harp on the negatives, you are keeping her down.
She has been given to you as a complement, a helper, a loving partner for life.
To move forward you must treat her as you want to be treated.
Being demeaning, unloving, and unkind separates families and friends, husbands and wives.

THINK BEFORE YOU SPEAK

What ever happened to being loving and kind?
Sadly we aren't as considerate of others feelings, I find.
Just thinking about ourselves just should not be.
Principled love, deep enough for others to see.
Fellow feelings and intense love from the heart.
Cold, cruel, and callous words, feelings of being beaten down, stabs like a dart.
In these critical last days, we all need each other,
We have to move forward and be united as brothers.
Necessary it is, to think before we speak.
Our personality and attitude should be humble and meek.
That always gives us something we can work on.
Putting others before ourselves, we aren't prone.
Our spiritual family are the last ones we expect to hurt us.
In them we want to be able to place our trust.

THIS BEAUTIFUL EARTH

So many lush beautiful places, on this earth.
From the clearest of waters on the coast, to the most breathtaking view of mountain ranges.
Incredible to ascend a mountain on a clear day.
You can see for miles and miles.
Homes down in valleys, along rolling hills, even on the sides of cliffs.
Gradually climbing higher and higher, but pay close attention to the clouds settling through the hills.
It gives you an enchanted feeling.
Peering off in the distance, above a peak is the endangered eagle.
Oh how majestic to watch.
Oceans so wide and calming.
Ripples, waves, and white caps over the waters.
Very few things compares to the true, natural beauty of the sea.
Looking at landscape while on the sea, is so intriguing.
There are hotels on the water that internal restaurants lights change every other night.
I recall seeing this once and it only added to the islands beauty.
The journey on the ocean proved to be lovely.
There are gardens and rain forest covered with flowers and fauna.
Thickets so green and lush, giving forth flowers of every description.
How it brightens an area.
The earth, so magnificent in itself, yet it is covered with so many awesome features.
It was given to man for him to enjoy.

THOUGHTS OF MY MOTHER

(dedicated to my mom, Catherine)

When I think about my mom,
I think of banana pudding with a hint more of cinnamon.
Smooth skin and almond complexion.
Two brilliant stars were her eyes, and a smile that could melt hearts.
If my mom was a coffee, she would be a cappuccino with all the froth.
A beauty mole adorned her face, that carried over to my niece.
Lovely in appearance and delicate as cotton candy.
She enjoyed trying new things like sherbet ice cream, or even peppermint patties.
Creative and able to make a delicious meal from the simplest of foods.
Absolutely an asset to anyone whose path she crossed.
Just as salt makes things more palatable,
She knew the right word to say at the right time.
As the net that lies beneath a trapeze artist, she was always there to catch you if you stumbled.
How graceful she carried herself, like the delicateness of a flamingo.
These are my thoughts of my mom I share with you.
Now share your thoughts of your mom with others, too.

TIME TO WONDER

I pause to wonder what happened to simple niceties.
No one says, "Please" or "Thank you" anymore.
People say anything they want to say and it doesn't matter how harsh it sounds.
Some things may be your right to say, but it doesn't mean that it is beneficial for you to say.
Other times, it may not be what you say, but how you say it.
Your demeanor, by facial or body, tells so much about YOU.
Never allow yourself to say one thing and your body language says something else.

TRANSITION OF THE DAY

Sitting here in my car,
Who are these I see from afar.
It must be someone's wife or another one's mother.
Then it may be someone's father or someone's brother.

Faces that depicts the deep stress of the day.
Nerves relaxed, and still others are frayed.
Did they ponder on the suns warmth on their faces
Or maybe that thought, not even in their minds trace.

Everyone rushing here and there.
Each day has it's own pressures and cares.
Before putting your vehicle in gear,
Take a moment to set your mind clear.

It's healthy to do this, I'm told.
A fresh and new inner peace is yours to hold.
Don't let go of it, grasp it tight.
Maintain this jubilant feeling with all of your might.

Completion of another day has come.
No more pounding the pavement, till your feet are numb.
You've reached your home where you reside.
Enjoy the evening with your family by your side.

TREES - UNSPOKEN BEAUTY

(Dedicated to June)

Have you ever watched trees on a clear Fall day?
Bowing and bending, just look at their sway.
Now add children to this scene at play.
Trees, with all their beauty has much to say.
Colors getting brighter; the greens and yellows.
This calming breeze easily changes to winds that bellows.
Nonetheless, the mood is so peaceful and mellow.
Short, stubby, slender, and yet others are stately fellows.
Trees with all their life seems to tell a story.
Much character they have, sometimes slow other times hurried.
We depend on them being around, we do not have to worry.
Some of them may give way under harsh weather's furry.
So much can be said about the beauty of a tree.
Take a moment and allow their serenity to set your spirit free.
They give so much to us if we just let them be.
Our lives depend on the oxygen they provide for you and for me.

TRUE BEAUTY

Often I give way to thoughts of this earth filled with beauty unlike what we see now.
Lingering memories of yesterdays sunset or maybe the beauty of flowers of every description.
If we just allow ourselves time to step back from the hurtful sights that engulf our daily lives, we will see so much more.
Sweet smelling trees of fruits so tasty, ripe and colorful, ready to eat.
Flowers, oh my, of every color and of every style imaginable. They dress up a lawn, a house, a park. Well anything that it surrounds.
Stately trees that were bare during the winter, now covered with foliage.
Of course never could we take for granted the warm breeze blowing against our skin.
The sky so full of lovely birds and now listen to how they sing to us.
I love being awakened in the morning by the sound of birds singing so cheerfully.
Farmland covered with new crops growing so fast. Plants gently swaying in the summer breeze. Have you ever seen a field of wheat blowing in the wind?
Their stalks bend and lean back and forth.
We are amidst a plethora of natural beauty that we take for granted every day.
But oh how different it would be if
There was none of this beauty around.
We are blessed with this expression of
God's love for us.

UNTITLED SNIPITS

There is always something positive in every situation if you look deep within.

*****

The light does get brighter at the end of the tunnel.
When you make it through, don't forget your friends that kept the torch burning to brighten your way

*****

A husband sees you at your wits end and can calm your very being with a warm touch and an endearing glance.

*****

Don't be so quick to judge your fellowman.
Step out of YOUR comfort zone and walk in his shoes.
Then just maybe you'll understand his anxiety.

*****

Being in love is like being tickled inside at the deepest point, by the softest of feathers.
You find yourself smiling for no apparent reason.
That sparkle in your eye is undeniable.

*****

Nothing can match the simplicity and the innocence of a child.
Their thoughts and life has not been tainted with generations of prejudices and bigotry.

*****

Nothing takes the place of a mothers love; it is sincere, heartfelt, and unconditional.

WHAT IS LOVE

Love is not just a feeling, but is a state of mind
Love is a joining of forces with a mate so endearing
Love causes you to place your mate before others
Love is all engulfing
Love reaches beyond outward appearances and treasures the true person from within

Love keeps you from letting him feel like he is last in your life
Love allows for errors and misunderstandings and your relationship flourishes
Love keeps you from thinking of those little personality differences as problems.
They are identity marks of your loved one
Love is that feeling in the pit of your stomach when you see, hear, or touch your loved one
Love brings out your intimate colors

Love gives you that feeling of security, inner peace, and satisfaction
Love makes you blossom and glow
Love should bring out the very best you are inside
Love is that yearning to share everything with a special someone
Love keeps you humble and selfless

Love and trust go hand in hand
Love is not picky, self-centered, or abrasive
Love is the healing force for a broken spirit
Love and respect are two intricate keys to any lasting relationship
Don't love him because you need him, need him because you love him
How wonderful when this quality leads to sharing your life forever with a precious mate

WHEN A MAN CRIES

We seldom see when a man cries.
Our tears are usually the ones he dries.
Men were created to handle pain.
Yet, showing their emotions, they refrain.
If he relates his concerns to you, he won't mind showing you when he's feeling blue.
Let him talk and get it off his chest, that always seem to work best.
Give him your hand on which to hold.
It will help him be strong, firm, and bold.
A man is here to hold us when we are stressed.
Disquieting thoughts he helps us to arrest.
That caring glance, soft words and listening ear, can help him see things more clear.
Men, too, have a sensitive side.
They want you in which they can confide.
Needed is our love and undivided attention.
Only then can he share his thoughts, without apprehension.

WHEN I AM OLD AND GRAY

Will you love me when I'm gray
As time goes by, day to day
Times and seasons change so fast
Yesterday was today, now it is in the past

The years have been kind to you
In many ways you have grown, but especially your love has grown too
When we said, "I Do", we became a single pair
With a love so pure, it is very rare

Nothing compares to the memories we have made
When stress and tensions arise, with you it soon fades
Now you feel like a comfortable old glove
Your love was sent from up above

So will you love me when I am old and gray
Deep down inside I feel you will, I must say
Body features maturing may seem strange
Working together, our love will never change

WHEN I

When I close my eyes, what do I see?
My handsome man who loves me.
When I stop to listen, what do I hear?
My passionate husband that I hold dear.
When I reach out my hand, what do I feel?
The gentleness of your touch revealed.
When I kiss your lips, what do I taste?
I taste my lovers sweetness without haste.
When I ponder on you, my senses come alive.
I come to appreciate you, who without, it would be difficult to survive.

WHILE YOU WEREN'T LOOKING - I WAS LOOKING AT YOU

So often I sit and watch you.
Nothing compares to pleasant expressions on your face.
It is almost as if you are smiling from within.
While you weren't looking, I was looking at you.

While having your dinner, I glance across the table.
You were enjoying your meal so much.
Inhaling every aroma and savoring every taste, you were.
While you weren't looking, I was looking at you.

Now our day has come to an end, and you give way to sleep.
You appear so comfortable and very much at peace.
And you are unaware of my gazing and pondering on you.
Yet, while you weren't looking, I was looking at you.

WHISPER TO ME SOFTLY

I love my time relaxing with you.
Sharing your space, now that we're no longer two.
Loving you, I feel so new.
Whisper to me softly.

How reassuring the safety of your arm.
Resting upon your chest, I feel no harm.
You make me feel all cozy and warm.
Whisper to me softly.

When I am home alone with you on my mind, without you, little peace can I find.
Upon my heart and soul your mark you've signed.
Whisper to me softly.

Reaching out to you to touch your face, outlining your eyes, your lips, and your nose, I trace.
Engulfed in your love my heart quickens its pace.
Softly I whisper to you.

Washing, cooking, and cleaning for you,
Mundane task but together, these we do.
Being in your life, my sad days are few.
Softly I whisper to you.

I love you. I do. I feel no pressure.
Your carrying me in your heart, I treasure.
Our love is without measure.
Whisper to me softly.
Softly I whisper to you.

WHO AM I? I AM WOMAN. I AM ME.

I am a woman complicated, yet simple.
I love deep conversations about life and love
I love walks on the beach or through a park to commune with nature.
I love watching heavenly bodies and meditating on the love our Creator has for us.

I am a woman shy, yet firm and bold.
I am quiet and shy when it comes to matters of the heart.
I feel very strong about matters of my God.
I feel courageous when my friends and family are in distress.

I am a woman so full of love to give, yet guarding my heart from unnecessary pain.
I enjoy the choice of being in love.
I enjoy giving of myself to my special someone.
I don't enjoy opening my heart up to hurt.

I am a woman creative and adventurous yet within reason.
Trying new things broadens my horizons.
Traveling to places far away expands my knowledge I have for learning a little about a lot of different Things.
Reaching out to others of national groups widens my love for my brothers.

I am a woman submissive and humble, yet stern and strong.
I am submissive to my husband taking the lead.
I am submissive to the headship of my mate.
I am strong and will not waver if it's against my conscience.

I am a woman reserved, yet also outgoing.
I do not love to be the center of attention.
I love sitting back and watching people.
I make it my business to converse with others.

I am a woman soft and gentle, yet able to say
NO when it is against my will.
Being touched by someone I love is pleasurable.
To caress the face or brows of a baby is enchanting.
A tender kiss, glance from afar, just melts my heart.

Who am I? I am Woman. I am Me.
I am a conglomerate yet I am an individualist.
I am a compilation of good gifts from our
Heavenly Father.
I am an anthology of years of many experiences.
I am a tower of strength, with God's power upon me.
WHO AM I? I AM WOMAN. I AM ME.

WHY CAN'T WE ALL JUST GET ALONG

Many times we often err.
It is not because we do not care.
Our first choice should be to treat others fair.
Some times we don't and more stress they bear.
We should treat each other as we want others to treat us.
Simply stated, it does build trust.
Handling misunderstandings should not be rushed.
Never do we want a persons heart to be crushed.
A weighty responsibility if we hurt someone.
Harsh words and actions all of us should shun.
Why can't we all together simply have fun?
Everyone in the human race are related, when all is said and done.
Love, kindness, and empathy goes a long way.
It can cover over those little errors by mistake we say.
Never do we want to hold our friends at bay.
We want a peaceful sleep and clear conscience at the end of the day.
So can we all just get along?
Forgive one another when we are wrong.
Lifts each other up when we need to be strong.
Because in the end, to each other we belong.

WILL YOU WALK ON

If you see me with a heavy heart
Feeling beaten down by the system
If you see me tattered and unkempt
With a face showing despair
Will you just walk on?

When I'm feeling loss and all alone
Feeling pushed aside and walked on
When I'm feeling depressed and
Struggling to remain sane
Will you just walk on?

As you pass me by and there's blankness on my face
As you pass me by and I'm physically
Showing pain of heart
Will you just walk on?

If you see me in a state
When I'm feeling really down and out
As you pass by and notice something is wrong
Please think twice before You Walk On.

WIND AND TREE CONNECTION

Often I stop and listen to the wind,
Or look at trees as they bend.
They seem to have a conversation of their own.
Especially groups of trees not just those standing alone.

The wind causes them to sway and bow as if to listen.
Leaves that after a rain, glistens.
Stately they stand, having strong roots.
Quietly they move, or sometimes they are mute.

Just look at the pine trees; they are so green.
Pine straw is put to good use so from that tree we glean.
As insulation around shrubs or bushes we place it,
We try to use it all, every little bit.

Their own fallen leaves serves as an insulator, too,
To help them grow tall and develop more leaves so new.
A constant cycle, we can't get above that.
But for now the yards are carpeted with leaves just like a huge mat.

YOU ARE ALWAYS IN MY HEART

How precious to have those in our lives that make the sun shine all the more brighter.
Someone whose smile warms and welcomes.
Someone so sincere and NEVER artificial.
You are who YOU are, a wonderfully loving person that I feel so blessed to have as my friend, confidant, and special companion.
Your spirit, so kind, and your demeanor so gentle.
I will forever love and cherish YOU.
Though miles apart, I carry you within my heart, always.

YOU'LL NEVER KNOW

You'll never know
When laughter turns to crying
You'll never know
When peace turns into fear
You'll never know
When good deeds turn into pitfalls
You'll never know
When a happy heart turns to a crushed spirit
You'll never know
When a mighty man turns to a cripple
You'll never know
When a living beauty turns into the ugly duckling
You'll never know
When a joyous occasion turns into a crisis
You'll never know
When peaceful silence turns to chaos
You'll never know
When a perfect day turns to disaster
You'll never know
When an optimist turns into a pessimist
However, attitude governs ones complete outlook on life.
Is the glass half full or half empty?
You govern how life is looked upon.
Use high insight and discernment and you WILL know.

YOUR HAND AND YOUR ARMS

The space between your fingers is there to hold my hand tightly.
I feel the clasp of an eternal grip.
Fingers intertwined that gives both of us a sense of support and strength.

The bend in your arm is to engulf me.
Wrapped around me, being wrapped around you.
That arm helps to keep me standing tall.
It means giving me confidence knowing you are there.

YOUR INNER FEELINGS

All your past wrong mistakes
All your future hopes and dreams to take

All your darkest deepest fears
All your bright and new ideas

All your doubts leave behind
All your love is forever mine

All your years that you have loss
All your time is mine, no cost

All your quirks, just let them be
All your good points, most never see

All your words said out of turn
All your respect I will assuredly earn

All your secrets you would never dare
All your desires you need to share

All your thoughts running through your mind
All your love will be mines to find

All your devotion will be for me
And for the "one" that set us free